Beginning Biographies

Paul Revere
American Patriot

Dwayne Hicks

PowerKiDS
press™

NEW YORK

Published in 2013 by The Rosen Publishing Group, Inc.
29 East 21st Street, New York, NY 10010

Book Design: Michael Harmon

Photo Credits: Cover (Revere), p. 19 SuperStock/SuperStock/Getty Images; cover (map) http://en.wikipedia.org/wiki/File:Lexington_Concord_Siege_of_Boston.jpg; p. 4 http://commons.wikimedia.org/wiki/File:PaulRevereByGilbertStuart.jpg; p. 6 Antonio Abrignani/Shutterstock.com; p. 7 www.ingetjetadros.com ©Ingetje Tadros/Flickr/Getty Images; p. 8 http://en.wikipedia.org/wiki/File:J_S_Copley_-_Paul_Revere.jpg; p. 9 cartela/Shutterstock.com; p. 10 Kean Collection/Staff/Archive Photos/Getty Images; p. 11 -Fotosearch/-Fotosearch/Getty Images; pp. 12, 18, 21 iStockphoto/Thinkstock.com; pp. 13, 14 UniversalImagesGroup/Contributor/Universal Images Group/Getty Images; p. 15 FPG/Taxi/Getty Images; p. 16 http://commons.wikimedia.org/wiki/File:Paul_Revere%27s_ride_-_NARA_-_535721.jpg; p. 17 © iStockphoto.com/BDPhoto; p. 20 © iStockphoto.com/gregobagel; p. 22 http://commons.wikimedia.org/wiki/File:Paul_Revere_1958_Issue-25c.jpg.

Library of Congress Cataloging-in-Publication Data

Hicks, Dwayne.
Paul Revere : American patriot / Dwayne Hicks.
    p. cm. — (Beginning biographies)
Includes index.
ISBN: 978-1-4488-8836-8 (pkb.)
6-pack ISBN: 978-1-4488-8837-5
ISBN: 978-1-4488-8599-2 (library binding)
1. Revere, Paul, 1735-1818—Juvenile literature. 2. Massachusetts—History—Revolution, 1775-1783—Juvenile literature. 3. Statesmen—Massachusetts—Biography—Juvenile literature. 4. Massachusetts—Biography—Juvenile literature. I. Title.
F69.R43H53 2013
974.4'03092—dc23
[B]
                                    2012011475

Manufactured in the United States of America

CPSIA Compliance Information: Batch #WS12RC: For further information contact Rosen Publishing, New York, New York at 1-800-237-9932.

Word Count: 452

Contents

A Famous American

Paul Revere is a well-known American. He lived a long time ago. Do you know what Paul did for America?

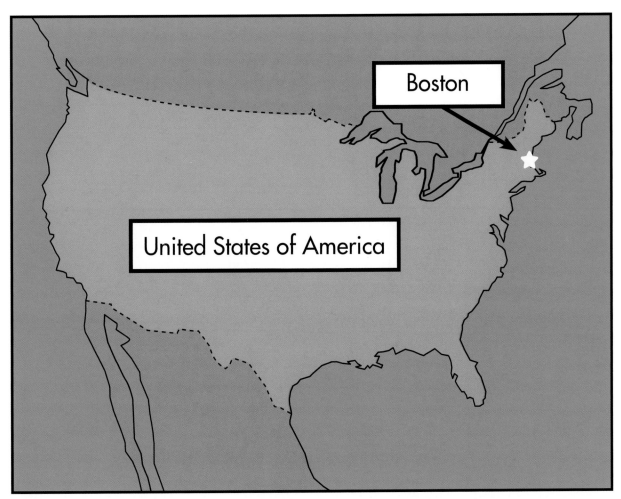

Paul was born in December 1734. He lived in Boston.

Boston was one of the first cities in the United States.

This is where Paul became **famous**.

Paul at Work

Paul went to school until he was 13, but then he left school to go to work. He was a silversmith. A silversmith makes things out of silver.

Paul's dad taught him to be a silversmith.

Paul worked in his dad's shop. They made things

like spoons and teapots.

Paul's dad died when Paul was 19 years old. Paul was the oldest son, so he had to take care of his family.

Paul took over his dad's business. The people in Boston loved his work. People still like his work today!

Paul also cut pictures and words into pieces of **metal**.

Then, he printed them on paper. He was a dentist, too.

Sometimes, he made fake teeth!

Paul joined the army in 1756. He made a lot of friends in the army. He and his friends did important things for our country.

The Midnight Ride

America was once made up of English **colonies**. This means that England was in charge of America. Many Americans didn't like this.

During this time, Paul was a messenger. He carried important messages to groups working to make America free. Paul rode his horse to get from town to town.

In 1775, Paul's friends learned that English **soldiers** were coming to stop the work for **freedom**. The soldiers wanted it to be a surprise.

Paul wanted to let everyone know. He rode his horse and told everyone the soldiers were coming. It was late at night, but Paul had to do it.

Paul rode his horse from town to town. He stopped
at every house. This job put Paul in a lot of danger, but
he wasn't scared. He wanted to help his friends.

Paul Revere's Path

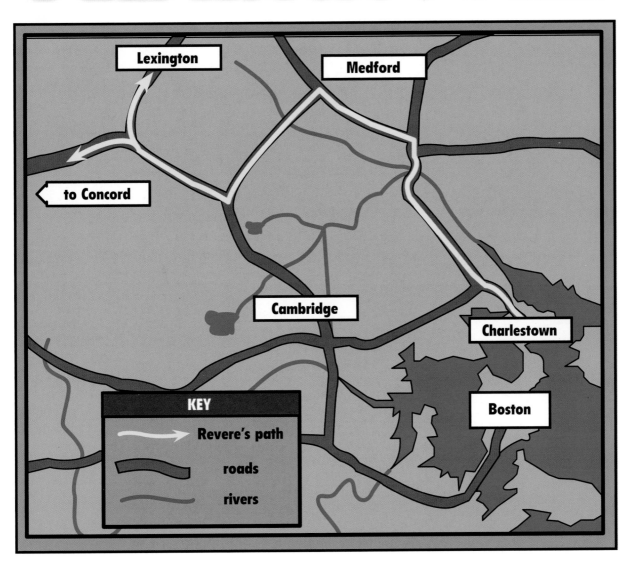

Lexington

Medford

to Concord

Cambridge

Charlestown

Boston

KEY

→ Revere's path

roads

rivers

Paul made his ride so he could help his country.
He knew he could get into trouble, but he wanted
to make America free. This makes him a hero.

After the war, Paul worked in his shop again. He worked as a silversmith for 40 years, but people remembered him for his ride.

Paul's Later Years

Paul had a good life and did a lot of important things. He loved his family. He had 16 children! He taught his sons how to work in his shop.

Paul died in 1818 when he was 83 years old. Years later, a man named Henry Wadsworth Longfellow wrote a **poem** about Paul's ride.

Paul Revere was a great American. He helped make the colonies free. We learn about Paul so we can remember our past.

Glossary

colony (KAH-luh-nee) Land that is owned by
   another country.

famous (FAY-muhs) Well-known.

freedom (FREE-duhm) The state of being free.

metal (MEH-tuhl) Hard matter that is shiny.

poem (POH-uhm) A kind of writing that has words
   that rhyme.

soldier (SOHL-juhr) A person who fights in the army.

Index

Due to the changing nature of Internet links, The Rosen Publishing Group, Inc., has developed an online list of websites related to the subject of this book. This site is updated regularly. Please use this link to access the list: www.powerkidslinks.com/bbio/paul